Pressed Petals

A Mother's Memories

JOY MORGAN DAVIS

PenPoint
PRESS

Dedication

Thank you, Mother ... for the gift of pressed petals.

Book design by Pat Molenaar

FIRST EDITION
Copyright © 2004
By Joy Morgan Davis
Published in the United States of America
By PenPoint Press
A Division of Sunbelt Media, Inc.
P.O. Drawer 90159 Austin, Texas 78709-0159
email: sales@eakinpress.com
website: www.eakinpress.com
ALL RIGHTS RESERVED.
1 2 3 4 5 6 7 8 9
1-57168-873-0
Library of Congress Control Number 2004113808

Perfectly Arranged

Memories, like the petals
From a gift of flowers,
Are pressed between
The pages of
My life . . .
Some sweet,
Some bittersweet,
Some stained
With tears . . .

But I remember that
The *bouquet* was
Beautiful!

Thank You, Lord, for the lovely arrangement!

Contents

The Gift of Pressed Petals 3
Unwilling Angel 5
My Son, The Graduate 11
A Child Shall Lead Them 13
The Composers 17
Ready for My Rainbow 18
Perfect Fit 20
"Amma" 21
Candles in the Dark 25
The Middle of a Miracle 26
God's Child 29
The Anthem 31
Who Loves You, Baby? 36
Where God Is 37
Landscapes 41
One Mother's Face 43
No More Tears 47
Heartstrings 49
Echoes 54
Wayward Child 55
Surprise! 58
Mother's Husband 59
A Red Rose 62

The Gift of Pressed Petals

My mother had died, and I, the only child, was left alone to close the windows and doors of her life, to lock the house and leave it empty of her.

I stood in her room that was flooded with so many long-ago emotions. The closets held decades of accumulation. The pigeonholes of her desk were filled with my letters to her. The bookcase was lined with history and literature and commentaries (for she was a teacher), and on the bottom shelf there was a row of college annuals, hers and my father's.

Curious, I sat crosslegged on the floor in front of them. I pulled out one, opened it . . . and caught my breath as a flutter of rose petals fell into my lap. There must have been a dozen or more, nearly transparent now, and I may have imagined it, but I thought I smelled a trace of fragrance.

In finding them so suddenly I felt a surge of delight, and longing, too. There was an overwhelming wish to know the girl who had pressed the petals there. A half century ago the girl who became my mother had saved a moment in time, a memory . . . of what? Of moonlight and roses? Of passion . . . tenderness . . . tears? Of some sunlit path that led to love? Or to a bittersweet goodbye? What had moved her heart to gather these petals and press them there, for time and eternity?

But the petals told no secrets. They were her memories, not mine.

And it came to me, as with great care I replaced the fragile remnants of an ancient rose, that memories, like the petals from a gift of flowers, are pressed between the pages of our lives. The fragrance lingers, and whenever the mind returns to that certain page we can recapture a moment in time that was so precious, so magical, so profoundly moving that we knew we must never forget.

Ever since that day when I found my mother's petals, I have consciously tucked away my memories from each treasured time, pressing them here and there between the pages of my life . . . so as to savor, and later relive, the myriad emotions of those moments I must never forget.

And frequently I whisper "Thank You" to my mother . . . for the gift of pressed petals!

Unwilling Angel

It was winter, the kind I'd never known before. The blizzard had blown into Michigan the week we arrived, and every day since had seen a new layer of snow. It was still snowing now, nine days later.

As I stood watching from an upstairs window, the best I could do for consolation was to remind myself how *noble* I'd been . . . but I wondered wryly if nobility was going to keep me all that warm!

I remembered the day my husband had told me about this three-month assignment in Michigan. "Let's all go," he said. "It'll be an adventure!"

He didn't want to be without us, and we certainly didn't want to be left alone, but the children were in the middle of school, braces, basketball. True, they were only seven and ten, but their schedules required a full-time chauffeur, secretary, and tutor, all named "Mom"!

"I'll try," I said bravely, and arranged my face into the facsimile of a smile.

Two weeks later I had gathered together records, report cards, and dental X-rays. I had talked by phone to a distant orthodontist, and to school officials. I had found fill-ins for my committees at church, school, and woman's club.

Then I began to pack. The facsimile of a smile fell. What

in the world would we wear in Michigan! We were from the Deep South. We wore cottons and linens all year long. I had seldom seen snow. The children had never seen it. I'd better shop! I had four days left.

Arriving in Michigan we moved into a rented house, completely furnished even to dishes and linens. The elderly couple who owned the house had gone to Florida for the winter. *Smart people!* I wished I were with them!

The first day of the blizzard my husband followed the snow plow to the plant. "No need for you to drive anywhere," he said. "Surely school will be out!"

Wrong! It was in!

"We want to walk," said my son excitedly. "It's only four blocks!"

He stood stuffed into his parka looking like Admiral Peary approaching the North Pole. His little sister looked up at him adoringly. She would have followed him anywhere, unafraid. Finally I let them go, certain I would never see them again. But they had come home, every afternoon, for five days.

Now it was Saturday morning, and the children had once again put on layers of clothes, earmuffs, mittens, and left for the little park at the end of our block. There was a frozen pond in the park, and people were half-skidding, half-skating across it.

Two hours passed. I was upstairs changing sheets, and feeling so sorry for myself. My husband's project kept him at the plant long hours, even on Saturdays. I was lonely. I missed my house, my friends, the choir. Besides, before this was over one of us was bound to catch pneumonia, or worse, and die.

I stopped and stood by the window. Every tree looked like a luminous Christmas tree, and the lawns were covered with a pure, pristine carpet. Well, it *was* pretty. You couldn't say it wasn't pretty.

Just then I saw the children. They were unmistakable in their bright parkas, almost tumbling toward the house, in and out of snowdrifts. But who was that with them! Another boy? I ran downstairs.

"Hi, Mom! This is Buddy! I found him at the park!"

For a moment I could only stare at Buddy. He was surely the most unkept child I had ever seen. His hair needed to be cut. His jacket was stained. His wool cap was two sizes too big. His wet mittens were stuffed into his back pocket, and his hands were red. His nose ran.

I was exasperated! What could the children have been thinking! This boy was obviously from another neighborhood, and from a very careless family, it would seem, to let him wander so far away.

As I closed the door behind the three of them, Buddy announced, "I been playin' with your boy at the park, so I come over here to see where you live!"

"Why . . . that's nice," I faltered. "But does your mother know where you are?"

"Oh, she don't care none! She works nights and sleeps days. I don't have to be home til suppertime!"

Suppertime? Good grief! It was only 11:00 A.M.! The children had brought him home for lunch!

As they settled in front of the fire, I set up snack trays facing the TV, where Superman was conquering the world. When I placed vegetable soup and cheese toast on Buddy's tray, he sat up straight. "Wowee! Thank *you*," he said heartily.

I sipped a cup of soup at the dining room table while I leafed through a magazine. Out of the corner of my eye I observed that Buddy's manners left a lot to be desired. His method of eating could best be described as "enthusiastic."

During the rest of the afternoon Buddy's "Wowee!" rang through the house. The children explored the basement, chased one another up and down the stairs, went outside for another romp. The second time they came in to warm up, Buddy spied my daughter's music books on the piano bench.

"I saw an organ once," he said. "It had long sticks under the bench that you push with your feet."

"That's true," I replied, hardly looking up from my magazine.

Buddy still held the music book. "I wish *I* could make an organ play," he said softly.

There was something about the way Buddy said this that caused me to take note. I smiled. "I've often wished the same thing, Buddy."

Then he was off again, upstairs to play "Sergeant" with a battalion of toy soldiers.

By now it was 4:00 P.M. and I was beginning to think of ways to get rid of Buddy. I wanted to put the house into some semblance of order before my husband returned home. What could I say? Surely there were chores to be done, homework waiting. That's what I would say . . . that my children had homework to do.

I made the suggestion as kindly as I could to the three of them, who were now stacking firewood to make a fort. They all agreed that they *did* have homework, . . . but please, before Buddy left, could they have hot chocolate in front of the fire?

I started to refuse, but it was such a simple request, and it *would* warm Buddy for the long walk home.

The cups of hot chocolate finally were drained, and the last of the marshmallows licked from the rims. Buddy started for the door, pulling on his stained jacket and the still damp mittens. The children and I followed him down the hall, and I was about to heave a sigh of relief.

Suddenly, with his small hand on the doorknob, he turned to my son, "Say! Your mom's an angel!"

I stood, frozen to the floor, the gracious compliment ringing in my ears. An angel? I, who had grudgingly given him soup and cheese toast, who silently had fussed over his manners, and fidgeted as he raced up and down my stairs! I, who had noticed his dirty shirt, but had not once seen his clear blue eyes? I, who had deplored his mother's carelessness, and never wondered what circumstances caused her to work through the long, weary night?

How *could* I have been so insensitive? I should have welcomed him, truly welcomed him! I should have encouraged him to talk more about the organ music, and told him the story of Handel and the "Hallelujah Chorus"! I should have given him more than a glance! *O Dear Lord*, my heart whispered, *I've overlooked one of the least of these!*

The door was open now, and my sudden tears felt cold on my cheeks. I hoped the children wouldn't notice. I bent down and put one arm around the ragamuffin, and the other around my son. "Come back any time, Buddy," I said.

He bounded down the steps and out into the snow. There he turned, and waved. His face was one big, beaming smile.

It was enough to give wings to an unwilling angel!

Epilogue

The little character, Buddy, has lingered in my heart all these years. We never saw him again after that one snowy day. But sometimes, when I'm watching other snowfalls, I remember Buddy . . . and I wonder if perhaps *he* was the angel!

My Son, The Graduate

Go West, young man, go West . . .
Like Duke Wayne
You will sit tall in the saddle
As you ride to take the sunset.

Success is yours,
And we send you to it . . .
Bravely, brightly,
With rightly arranged smiles
On our faces,
Looking at you
With the love and logic
That tells us you are
Wise and wonderful
And grown in grace
And ready, O yes,
Ready!

And so you go
Galloping toward life
As we stand
Waving wildly,
Shouting our goodbyes . . .

While hid behind my heart
There is the sad, insistent
Whisper . . .
Come back, young man, come back.

A Child Shall Lead Them

I learned a life-lesson one day: You don't have to wait until you need to move a mountain to talk to God. He can move molehills, too!

I've had a few PROBLEMS in my life, but mostly I've had problems, in little letters. Not that these don't matter. They do. In terms of wear-and-tear they work like the slow erosion of the sea on a sandcastle. Finally the sandcastle is washed away, and with it the dreams and plans and promises.

But still I was always reluctant to pray about the "little letter" problems. Perhaps on a dreary day I might shed a tear or two and begin to talk to the Lord about my load of care. But then I would remember all the old admonitions. "Count your blessings," they said in Sunday school. "Look at what you *have* instead of what you have not," they counseled. "Think of the people who are hungry, or in hospitals, or in prison! Now *that* is trouble," I was reminded.

And so timidly I would take back my burden from the throne of grace in order to give the Lord more time to deal with the really big issues, like plague and pestilence or sin and shame!

Then one day my daughter, my charming child who has turned into a winsome, wise young woman, put it all in place for me! Drew Ann has a degree in psychology, and so she is our family "sage." Actually she was something of a sage before she went away to college. Even as a child she would startle us with her clear conceptions of people's feelings, their motivations, their meanings. She can "read between the lines" better than anyone I know. Her interest in psychology was natural, for, simply put, it is an interest in people and their needs. Other children are natural tennis players, or mathematicians, or musicians. Drew Ann *understands.*

On this day we were driving into the city. Drew Ann was at the wheel. She does not trust me to drive and talk at the same time, and since it is folly to imagine my not talking during a trip of more than ten minutes, she was driving.

On the freeway we fell into a discussion about one of my day-to-day dilemmas, a situation for which there seemed to be no solution. It was a relationship with a relative, a relationship with which I had lived for a long time. Like the sea on the sandcastle, it was wearing me away. We talked about the cycle of emotions which created the dilemma over and over again. The cycle just kept repeating itself, unpleasantly. It wasn't a life or death situation, but there seemed to be no end to it, and I was discouraged. Oh, more than that. I was at my wit's end!

Soon we were in the center of the city, surrounded by cars and horns and signal lights. As we waited for a light to change from red to green, a mass of humanity crossed the street in front of us, hurrying, scurrying about their business. Suddenly, in the midst of all that humanity, we saw a young woman. She was about Drew Ann's age. She had lovely light hair and a clear complexion. She was beautifully dressed. She carried a small leather briefcase, obviously a bright young businesswoman in the professional world.

She was also crippled. One of her legs was twisted, bent in the wrong direction under her, making it shorter than the other. She limped in a loping stride, one shoulder forced forward by the deformity. Her face was set purposefully on the light, so that she would be sure of getting across the street before it changed.

My heart melted, and my eyes grew misty. She was so beautiful, so successful. She had overcome such impossible odds, and now competed in a world full of people who could walk without thinking. She was also somebody's daughter!

"Oh, how brave and beautiful she is," I murmured. "And how it must break her mother's heart to see her struggle for every step. Now *there* is trouble! I don't *have* any troubles!"

Drew Ann reached over and patted my hand. "That's right, Mom. She has a *big* problem, and you have a *little* problem. But don't discount it! It can be significant!"

I was startled. *Significant.* What an interesting word! Surely I had assumed I was *in*significant! I had been timid with my tiny trouble. I was wrong!

Drew Ann continued. "I've often observed this attitude when people are troubled. They think they should handle some little thing, because it *is* a small thing. But from what I've seen and read and studied in my classes, little things can become big things overnight if left to our human hands alone. They can't be taken lightly just because they're little. They should be seen as significant, and dealt with as such!"

She was right, of course. Whether in psychology or theology, things should not be taken lightly. Indeed, God does not take them lightly.

"I know when the sparrow falls," He said. And if His eye is on the sparrow, then I know He watches me!

I smile as I remember . . . it was my child who led me to realize that He listens, and loves even me!

The Composers

Dear Lord . . .

Little Anna lay in my arms,
One week old and wonderful,
And suddenly I wanted
To sing!
No matter that
I can't carry a tune
Or hold a note
Or harmonize . . .
There was music
In me . . .
Music!

This must be what it means
To have a
Song in my heart.

O, let's don't stop with
A song, Lord . . .
Let's do a
Symphony!

Ready for My Rainbow

I was standing at the kitchen counter, putting together a meatloaf, chopping onions and bell peppers. In the middle of the floor sat my four-year-old son. He had always been a serious child. Even as a baby he would solemnly study the world, as if wondering how it worked. He gave meticulous attention to whatever he did, placing his blocks in exact rows, and insisting that his toy cars "stop" at the STOP signs of his imagination.

Today he was playing with a large plastic boat. It was his Noah's Ark for the day. He loved the story of the flood, with all those animals floating merrily along. He always drew a rainbow over every picture in his coloring books. And he was fascinated with rain. He would stand at the window, watching it. Once he asked me if the clouds had a zipper that God could pull to let the water out.

So today he was playing "Noah"! He had a shoe box full of little plastic animals and tiny toys, and with great concentration he was putting the animals, two at a time, into his ark. He put in tiny dolls for Noah's "little girls," and miniature cars for Noah's "little boys," and everything had to fit exactly so.

On the counter beside my meatloaf was a small radio. I was paying very little attention to the program, but there was an evangelist coming over the airwaves, who was preaching a stem-winder. That man was fervent! And loud! And about halfway through his sermon, in fine oratorical form he shouted, "WHAT, I ask you . . . WHAT can clean up this old world!"

As he paused briefly for breath, the four-year-old at my feet looked up at the radio and said decisively, "A soapy flood would do it!"

I looked at him, and laughed out loud! What an absolutely simple solution! Suddenly, I got a mental picture of God, somewhere up there, with a big box of Tide, adding soap suds to His flood! What a wash day!

That was many years ago, but in the passage of time since, I have thought of that little boy's comment often as I have watched Christians face the floods of life . . . floods of pain and disappointment, floods of great grief, floods of loss and loneliness. And so often the cry is, "O, Lord! It's been raining in my life long enough! I'm so ready for my rainbow!"

I've watched the rain in my own life, and in the lives of others, and I've seen it rain for forty days . . . or forty months . . . or sometimes longer.

But God's hand will one day draw a rainbow over every stormy sea, for it is His promise . . . His beautiful, breathtaking, awe-inspiring promise! And God's promises are forever!

A Perfect Fit

You were so little,
Standing there enveloped
In your father's coat and hat,
The tie touching your toes.
"Look," you said,
"I'm like Daddy!"

Oh, yes, my son,
You are!
You've grown
Into his clothes,
And you've taken on
His tender ways . . .
For as a child
You wore more than
His coat and hat . . .

You were covered
In his love!

"Amma"

Amy Carmichael was born in Northern Ireland in a lovely home where she was raised to be a "proper lady." There were fervent Christian influences in her life, and at an early age she felt God's leadership to foreign missions.

She arrived in India in 1895, to work with other missionaries in the villages of Southern India. The pagan conditions there were appalling. There was a stigma attached to having too many girl babies, and so frequently these precious little ones were simply left at the edge of the jungles to die, often to be eaten by wild animals.

Amy's heart was broken one day as she came upon one such abandoned baby, just a few hours old. She picked it up and carried it close to her heart while, over a few days, she brought the baby back from the brink of death. Soon she knew what she wanted to do. She would establish a home for the abandoned babies, and give them protection, care, and comfort.

As her mission for abandoned babies grew, she was soon aided by native nurses, doctors, and lay Christians. The work was called Dohnavur Fellowship, named after the village in which it was located. Only a few years later, Dohnavur was not only an orphanage for babies, but a school with dormitories for older children, and a hospital fully staffed by native physicians.

As the little ones grew, they began to call Amy "Amma," the Indian word for "Mother." She who had never married, who had never given birth, was suddenly surrounded by children who looked to her for the love of a mother, and she gave it generously to each one. There was always enough to go around! She was, in all matters of the heart, a *mother*!

And then, after thirty years in India, Amy was involved in a serious accident which left her crippled and in pain for the last twenty years of her life. During those twenty years she was barely able to leave her bed. She lived in the center of the Dohnavur campus, and could watch from her wide windows all the activities, and the children coming and going.

By now, many of her children were grown and scattered throughout India. A number of them were poised and educated and had attained high positions. But still they wrote to their Amma, the only mother they had ever known. Many of their letters, and hers to them, have been collected and published in several books, most notably *Candles in the Dark*.

The trust that these grown children had in Amy's warmth and wisdom is evident over and over again, as they poured out their hearts on the pages. They shared with her their joys and sorrows and their dilemmas. And always she answered, offering courage and care, sometimes adding admonition or advice, often suggesting scriptures that would inspire faith and fortitude.

Even as her health drained away toward the end of her days on earth, she continued to write to her children.

On the last day of her life, she was found at twilight-time, propped up on her pillows, her pen and writing pad still in her hands.

She had begun a letter to a young man who had written his Amma, telling her of a dark, discouraging time in his life. He was desolate, and searching for some assurance that God still cared.

The last words Amy Carmichael ever wrote were to this young man. She had finished only one sentence before she died.

That sentence was, *"If so dear to me, what to Him!"*

I have carried those words in my heart ever since I first read them. As a mother, those words enabled me to lay my head on my pillow at night and sleep peacefully. For after I had, in prayer, pleaded for my children, I remembered, "If they are so dear to me, *what to Him!*" In prayer I can take to the Throne of Grace my pleas, and thankfully then I can *leave* them there! God's love is so breathtakingly BOUNDLESS!

I once heard a world-famous gospel musician, Frank Boggs, sing a simple spiritual:

He's got the whole world in His hands!
He's got you and me, Brother, in His hands.
He's got the tiny little babies in His hands.
He's got the saints and the sinners in His hands.
He's got the whole world in His hands!

And He's got my children in His hands—to counsel them, to console them, to guide them through the trials of this imperfect and fault-filled world—and they are dearer to Him than they are to me.

I remember Amma's words . . . and I rest!

Candles in the Dark

It's so dark,
Lord,
And my candles
Are so few . . .
Could You hurry up
The dawn?

In time, Child,
In time . . .
Dawn is never early,
But it's never late either!
Meanwhile, I've counted
Your candles . . .

Your supply is
Sufficient!

In the Middle of a Miracle

I remember that it was my favorite story. As a child I asked for it over and over at bedtime. I always listened with the same sober fascination, for the main character was a child, like me, in the middle of a miracle!

My mother would paint the word pictures for me: the sunlit Sea of Galilee, the smooth blue water, the small boat. Jesus had gone out on the lake to be alone. But when He returned to shore He found that the crowds had followed Him. They had been watching Him for days as He healed the lame and the blind, and even raised Lazarus from the grave. Now throngs of people crowded around Him as He walked from the shore to the gentle slopes surrounding the sea.

When He turned to face them they sat down, spreading their colorful cloaks all over the hillside. They were completely captivated as He spoke to them of peace and compassion and rest for the weary. All day long they listened, and did not leave. At last the sun began to set, but still they stayed, wanting to hear every word He said.

Soon the disciples began to worry. They looked at the throngs of people—thousands, the Bible says—and wondered what they would eat at the end of the day, for they were far from any town. But it was then that a lad came to

Jesus and offered Him his lunch, five small loaves of bread and two fish. And suddenly that child was in the middle of a miracle! Jesus broke the bread and fish into pieces, and in Jesus' hands that lunch was multiplied to feed a throng of thousands, with baskets of food left over!

When I was little, listening to the story, I would wish that the lad was my friend. I would wish that I could ask him what it was like, to sit at Jesus' feet, to see his lunch in Jesus' hands, to be in the middle of a miracle.

But now that I am grown, I wish his mother was my friend. Now as I hear the story, still with the same fascination, I want to know about the mother. She and I have so much in common, you see. I, too, am the mother of a lad!

This mother seems anonymous at first glance. Her name is never mentioned, nor her age. We know nothing of her nature. Did she chatter cheerfully as she went about her work? Did she sing? Was she silent? It doesn't matter, for in my mind I see the imprint of her sandals all through this story. On that day she would have risen early to mix the dough, to roll it into little loaves, and bake it in an earthen oven. Then she would have rested underneath the arbor behind the house. Her boy would awaken and find her there, and together they would drink the fresh goat's milk, and eat the fruit and cheese and bread she had prepared. And then she would have packed the lunch.

I wish so much that I could ask her what she thought as she prepared to send her son to follow Jesus that day. After all, to many He was a roving rabble-rouser. But this mother had perhaps seen Him for herself. She would have seen He was a man of strong physique, with the powerful arms and calloused hands of a carpenter. And she would have observed His personality. He had a blazing indignation that denounced the wrongs He saw in the world. And yet when the children came to Him, there was such a tenderness in His touch as He took them on His knee. He was, in fact, all the things she wanted her son to be.

And so she wrapped the bread and fish together, gave them to the lad, and said, "Today, my son, I want you to follow Jesus. Listen well to His words. Learn His ways!"

That mother and I are soulmates, of sorts. For I, too, live with my son in a world full of wrong. There is hunger and homelessness. There is always a war somewhere on earth. Communism has turned whole nations faithless. For multitudes, freedom is fleeting. Our leaders often lie. Our trust is often betrayed. My son will face fear and confusion on all sides. He must be able to stand tall against temptation. He will need to be wise, and just, and gentle. Most of all he will need to know the Lord, if he is to live in this world with any measure of peace.

And so I will give him all I can, my care and counsel, my time, my attention. And then I will mentally pack up my love, place it in his hands, and say, "Go, my son, and follow Jesus!" It's the only way I know to be sure the love will last a lifetime.

And it's the only chance he'll ever have to be in the middle of a miracle!

God's Child

At ten years old,
Amber's tiny shoulders were
Too small to bear the burdens
Of the world . . .
But she tried!

When Julie and Jeanie
Refused to play the game
Together,
She pulled them from the
Separate sides of the room . . .
"Please kiss and make up,"
She pleaded.

When John Robert
Spilled his fingerpaints
And left the table in a temper

She followed him . . .
"At least you made a picture,"
She soothed.

When on Picnic Day
It rained and the class
Sat gloomily inside
With their sandwiches,
She walked to the window . . .
"But the flowers look delighted,"
She observed.

I watched,
Remembering . . .
Blessed are the peacemakers,

For they shall be called
The children of God.

The Anthem

Amber and William, our first two grandchildren, always lived way-away from us. And so each summer from the time they were three and five they came to us for a two-week visit. And for two weeks I was the Camp Director! Each morning, after breakfast on the patio, we left the house for the day's "Activity."

We visited the zoo to see the "effelants." We rode the trolley cars. We toured Mrs. Baird's Bakery. We went to the Science Museum's "Light and Electricity" show, where one on-stage experiment made Amber's long blonde hair stand straight up. We saw the Iron Horses, and watched a film about how they were made. We studied Japanese Gardens in the big *Britannica*, and then drove to Fort Worth to walk through a real Japanese Garden and practice being "peaceful." One weekday morning we visited the silent sanctuary where their parents were married, and for half an hour they played "wedding." Amber was the bride, marching solemnly down the aisle, and William was the preacher, giggling through the entire ceremony.

One day there was to be an eclipse of the sun. We followed instructions in the newspaper to make cardboard "glasses" to view the eclipse through a pinhole. And then on the living room floor we laid out the universe with plates of different sizes. William was the sun, holding a yellow cake platter. Amber was the moon, with a silver cookie tray. We arranged the planets around the sun, and "walked through" the movements that caused the eclipse, while Grandfather, the engineer, instructed us from the encyclopedia. (I don't know how much science they learned, but for an hour they were part of God's distant worlds.)

They had been introduced to art at an early age. Amber was ten, when walking through a museum she exclaimed, "Oh, there's a Georgia O'Keeffe!" They had also been raised with music, especially choir music. Their mother was choir president in their church, and they were more than familiar with anthems that sang of God's honor and glory!

After our "Activity" for the day, we came home at 2:00 for naps—at least Grandmother took a nap. I'm not sure they snoozed, but they were supposed to stay in their separate rooms for an hour. And then to finish the afternoon we went to play in the pool until it was time for Grandfather to come home from work.

They were fascinated with the tall buildings in downtown Dallas, and often after dinner they would persuade Grandfather to "drive down between" the buildings, and then stop at the hotel which had an ice cream bar.

But our most dramatic moment of any summer happened at the pool.

William was five years old, a strong, sturdy little boy. Amber was seven and could swim. I was . . . well, I was older and could not swim, but I could traverse the length of the pool in no time on my innertube.

There were several innertubes in the pool, and a long "float." William had walked out to the end of the diving board, though he had been well instructed not to jump into the deep water. But at that moment the long "float" floated by, directly at the end of the diving board. In his five-year-old mind, he thought the float always stayed on top of the water . . . and the moment was too tempting! He jumped, expecting the float to catch him. It caught him, all right, and promptly sank beneath his weight. He bobbed to the surface, went under, and bobbed up again.

Amber was screaming, "GRANDMOTHER! William is drowning!"

I was running around the edge of the pool with my innertube, about to plunge in after him, when I saw to my amazement that he was dogpaddling furiously toward the side of the pool, and making good time! He reached the edge just as I did, and I pulled him out, sputtering and spewing and wailing all at the same time. Amber brought a towel and we wrapped him up and held him tight until his tears subsided.

I was thinking, "What do I do now?" I wanted him to know that he should never throw himself into deep water again. But I also didn't want him to be forever afraid of water.

Finally, I picked him up and carried him to the steps in the shallow end of the pool. The three of us sat on the steps, in the water, with William still on my lap.

I said, "Now we know we must not ever go into the deep water again until we can swim. But we also want to thank God for William's amazing strength and courage, to paddle his way to safety!" Then we bowed our heads and had our prayer of thanksgiving.

The rest of the day passed easily and uneventfully until it was time for goodnight stories. I read to the children from a big Bible storybook that had been mine as a child. And after the story, it was time for bedtime prayers.

I prayed.

Amber prayed.

And then it was William's turn. He thanked God for his parents, his playmates, the missionaries . . . and then he remembered the pool.

"And thank You, God," he said in a sturdy voice, "for my strength and courage . . . *and for my honor and glory!*"

I just had to peek! There was Amber, eyes squeezed tightly shut, her mouth spread out in a wide grin. But it was William's face that was the sight to behold. With hands folded under his chin, his face was turned upward, fairly glowing with fervent faith and gratitude.

And in that moment I saw that God had blessed the little face, truly, with Honor and Glory!

Who Loves You, Baby?

I saw him
Running toward me,
The son of my son,
Four years old and flying . . .
"Look at me, Granmudder!
  I'm a bird
  I'm a plane
  I'm Superman!"

He climbed the ladder
To the top of the slide,
Balancing briefly . . .
"Look at me, Granmudder!"
  As he skidded headlong
  Down the silver slope.

He tumbled, topsy-turvy,
Into the pool
Sputtering,
His arms spinning in wide
Cartwheels . . .
"Look at me, Granmudder!
  I'm a motorboat!"

Oh, son of my son,
Who loves you, Baby?

"Granmudder!"

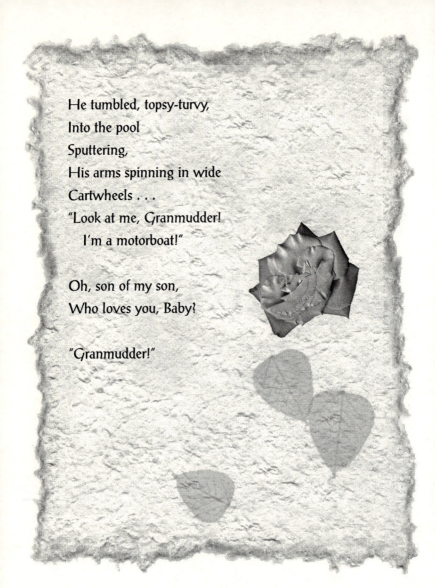

Where God Is

Our delightful daughter-in-love, Shannon, called: "I'm about to do something that will TOTALLY CHANGE MY LIFE! But it's a secret, and I can't tell now!" (She sounded enthusiastic, so we assumed she was not about to join the French Foreign Legion, or some such.) Yet we could not imagine what could be so earth-shaking as to change her life, TOTALLY!

For several months we waited, wondering when the "something" was going to happen. Finally the call came, this time from our son. "We're adopting a baby!" he said excitedly. "And she's going to be born next week!"

I had to sit down. Adopting?! A baby?! What on earth were they thinking! They already had two perfectly good children to which Shannon had given birth, a girl, fourteen, and a boy, twelve. They were long past 2:00 A.M. feedings, twenty diapers a day, colic, and constant calls to babysitters. Where had this daunting idea come from?!

From their hearts, it seemed. They explained that they had always wanted a family of three, and since Shannon could not give birth again, they had decided to have a baby anyway. They would adopt!

However, much easier said than done, when you're thirty-six and thirty-seven years old. The situation is that there are not enough babies, and too many couples in their twenties who want one of them. Calls and contacts to agencies in the metroplex had proven futile. Our son is a physician, and he finally resorted to word-of-mouth in the medical community. That produced results. Soon there was someone who knew of a baby to be born . . . a baby which would be given up for adoption. They were ecstatic! And now all the legalities had been handled and the baby was due! Furthermore, she was to be born in Dallas!

All that day we sat by the phone, waiting for it to ring. If the baby came early in the day, we hoped to dash over to the hospital and get a glimpse of her before she left for West Texas.

No such luck. Our son's lawyer, his legal secretary, and a family friend had come for the baby. They spent the day signing and receiving official papers, and finally had to dash for the airport to catch a 5:00 plane for home. They handed the pilot written medical permission to fly with a newborn, and settled into their seats.

As soon as the plane was airborne, to their surprise the flight attendant picked up her microphone. "Ladies and gentlemen," she said, "I want to announce that Amy Elizabeth Davis is on board today, flying to meet her new parents . . . and at less than twenty-four hours old, she is the youngest passenger ever to fly on this airline!"

The passengers broke into applause. Amy managed to sleep through the commotion! But it was only the beginning.

As the plane landed and the passengers filed into the airport, there stood a welcoming committee: Amy's parents, her brother and sister, other friends of the family, and a collection of colored balloons. The lawyer handed Amy to our son, who promptly lost his composure and began to weep as the little family joined in a group hug. Cameras clicked all around. By this time they had been surrounded by the passengers from the plane, all eager to see Miss Amy Elizabeth Davis, less than a day old!

What a love this child has been to us . . . blonde hair, blue eyes, cherubic face, and a personality that puts us all in the shade. And every time we look at her, we are reminded of God's goodness . . . His miraculous plan for her and for us, to make us a family!

Once a young woman with a yearning heart prayed:

I want to touch You, Lord!
I know You're there . . .
But sometimes I need
   Something tangible,
   Something I can hold to, cling to,
   Something I can put my arms around,
   Something I can *see!*

Then go, Daughter . . .
Find a child who needs
   The tears wiped away,
   Hurts kissed and made well,
   Fears calmed . . .
Touch the child
And you will touch Me . . .

For inasmuch as you have
Put your arms around one of
The least of these,
You have also
Held Me!

Landscapes

There are twenty years
Between the two . . .
My child
And my child's child.
Twenty years between
Two children who are the
Dear, delight of my life . . .
My pleasure
My treasure
My love . . .
Each child the same!

But in *me* a miracle occurred . . .
A metamorphosis!
I am no longer "Mother"
With a thousand things to sort . . .
With hurried, worried, weary
Days and nights,

Sometimes losing sight of love
In the avalanche of
Meals, manners, measles,
Costumes for the Christmas pageant,
And sudden adolescence . . .

I am "Grandmother"!

I hug without hurry.
I talk.
She listens.
I spin old-time tales
Like long threads linking
Our lives
Generation to generation.

I rest . . .
The large, looming mountain
Of responsibility is moved . . .

And I can see the scenery
Of love.

One Mother's Face

Madame Charlotte Bartholdi was a wealthy widow of France. She lived on a large estate in the small city of Colmar, in Alsace-Lorraine, with her two sons. She was the mother-matriarch of the estate, commanding her staff of servants and workmen with a benevolent hand. And to her sons she was the strong center of their lives.

Both boys were artistic, and Madame Bartholdi gave them every educational advantage. The older brother became a painter in Paris. The younger brother, Auguste Bartholdi, became a sculptor, winning worthy accolades while still a youth. One of his first acclaimed works was done immediately after the American Revolution, during which France sent men, munitions, and money to secure our victory. Auguste had created a maginificent statue of General Washington and General LaFayette, with the flags of the two nations furled around them. It had attracted worldwide attention as artists from around the world flocked to see it, and other works by Bartholdi.

And so it was, on an evening in 1865, that a group of politically influential Frenchmen invited the acclaimed sculptor to dinner. They had a purpose in mind.

The American Civil War had just ended, and this nation had survived to become the "united" states. The French people also wanted this kind of strength and stability in government. And so these wealthy men, all committed to this dream, decided that it would be an inspiration to the population if France was to give to America some symbolic gift, a gift that would declare to the world that France would one day also have a government of the people, for the people, and by the people! They had determined that the gift should be a statue, of significant size, a Statue of Liberty! And they wanted Auguste Bartholdi to design it.

The dinner that evening was an emotional one, as one by one men spoke fervently of freedom for the common man, and Auguste accepted their commission with the zeal of a Christian on crusade. It was a task that would take a decade of dedication to finish.

The sculptor began at once to sketch possible designs. He worked feverishly, discarding dozens of sketches over the first few weeks.

Finally, on his first sea-crossing to America, there came the morning when his ship sailed into New York's harbor. Standing on deck in the early morning mist, he watched the skyline of Manhattan rising with the sun, as the ship passed a small island in the harbor. The island had once been the site of a fort, but now all that remained was the granite foundation of the fort, in the shape of a star, where each point had held a battlement. Bartholdi was admiring the artistic shape of the old granite star, when at that very moment a ship of emigrants, on course for Ellis Island, sailed by. Bartholdi saw on deck the mass of emigrants, in their dark European clothing, their faces lifted in wonder and hope toward the new world. And suddenly he was seized with inspiration!

The Statue of Liberty would be a lady, standing in the center of that old granite star! She would hold high a light which would never grow dim! She would be destiny! Uphold her, and men would live. Reject her, and men would die, as surely as the slave never truly lives. Indeed, the Statue of Liberty had been born!

As the design took shape over the next several months and neared the time when the actual sculpting would begin, Bartholdi needed a model. His search was simple. He would use the two women in his life, his wife, and his mother. His wife was the beautiful Jeanne Emilie, and he used her graceful arms and hands . . . but for the face . . . for the face he wanted character, courage, conviction. A woman approachable, but powerful. And as he thought of his mother's life he remembered her commanding personality, her benevolence, and most of all, her conviction.

One instance of her convictions stood out in his mind. It was during the Franco-Prussian war. Madame Bartholdi was distressed when the French royals literally blundered their way into this war. She knew that the French army, made up of aristocrats who wore velvet uniforms, would be no match for the Prussians, who were born military strategists. She took the train from Colmar to Paris and talked to everyone of importance, urging them to stop the hostilities before all of France was overrun.

It was too late, for the Prussian army was by now

marching methodically across Alsace-Lorraine. They took Colmar without a shot being fired, and chose the Bartholdi estate as their headquarters. Madame Bartholdi was, at that time, free to leave and go to her sons in Paris. But she refused to desert her home, her city, and her beloved Alsace-Lorraine in the hands of the invaders. She would not leave the house!

The Prussian general confined her to a third-floor suite of rooms, and allowed her to walk in the gardens once a day. And there she stayed, a virtual prisoner in her own home, for several years until the occupation of Alsace-Lorraine ended.

Auguste Bartholdi saw in his mother's face what he wanted for his statue—the face was fervent, refined, commanding, compassionate! And thus it was that one mother's face came to be carved on the most famous statue in the world.

On the day of dedication in October of 1886, President Grover Cleveland rose to give the final address. He closed with these words: "We will not forget that Liberty has made her home here. We will love her, and lift her up, until her bright light has reached around the world!"

What a Lady! And it is a mother's face that reflects the freedom we hold dear!

No More Tears

When I was small
My mother had two
Simple solutions to
Everything . . .
Cinnamon tea and
Bubble baths.
There was no problem which
Could not be solved with
One or the other.

If it was winter
And things went wrong,
We had a cup of tea.
If it was summer
And I had a sad day
She'd say, "Let's have a
Bubble bath!"
And as the frothy foam rose
Around me she'd sing . . .
"Bubble, Bubble, *Double* Bubble,
Take away my toil and trouble". . .

And soon my tears would be
Forgotten.

Often then she'd tell me . . .
"In heaven there's a shining river,
And when we have crossed *those* waters
God will take away our tears
Forever!"
It sounded wondrous to me then,
And it sounds wondrous to me
Now!

It's been half a century
Since my childhood,
But I still resort to bubble baths
On sad days . . .
And as the turmoil of my mind
Melts away, I think . . .
If a simple bubble bath can bring
This much comfort,
I can't wait to wade in
Those wondrous waters
Where my tears will be
Forever forgotten . . .

How heavenly!

Heartstrings

She was eighty, my mother, still spry with a spring in her step, when she attended a reunion of her college classmates on the campus of Mississippi College in Clinton, Mississippi. She lived just ten miles away in the state capital, Jackson, and was often on the campus in Clinton. But the reunion each May was a special time to which she always looked forward with great anticipation. Amazingly, many of her classmates were still alive "and kickin'," she would say.

This May the reunion was no different—lots of hugs and hellos, lots of laughter, lots of pictures pulled from patent leather purses to show off grandchildren, great-grandchildren, vacations taken, new condos bought when "the old home place" was sold. It was a great get-together!

Finally, midafternoon, after a day of festivities, this eighty-year-old Campus Queen got into her little red Nova to cross the highway to the president's mansion on the hill, where she was to serve at an afternoon tea. And it was then that this dear little lady drove through an obscure stop sign and into the path of an eighteen-wheeler. She lived just two weeks in Intensive Care, and then God, in His goodness, took her home.

And I was suddenly an orphaned "only child." I cried

desolately. Not for her, in glory, but for myself! Suddenly, I wasn't FIRST on anybody's list anymore. My husband loves me, but men are always out conquering the world, and that tends to take a lot of their time and attention. My children love me, but they have lives and loves of their own. When they wake up every morning, I am not usually the first thought on their minds, nor should I be.

But I knew that every morning, when my mother opened her big brown eyes, her first thoughts were of me, her only child—and that then those thoughts were turned into prayers. My mother's prayers were a mainstay of my life. I knew they were personal and specific to my needs. And I knew something else. I knew my mother often prayed for me with many tears. How did I know that? She never said so. I knew, because I often pray for *my* children with many tears. Not that their lives have been problematic; indeed, they give us pride and pleasure daily. But when a mother prays for her child, the heartstrings between herself and that child tug so tenderly . . . and the heart fills up and spills over . . . and the tears come as she pleads before the Throne of Grace for God to give that child strength and courage and His compassion for whatever the child will face on that day.

I knew my mother prayed for me that way, and when she died I felt ABANDONED! I remember thinking, perhaps I can learn to live without her presence, but how will I live without her prayers?

One day, God gave me a mental picture—perhaps the prophets would have called it a vision—but it was just a mental picture. Suddenly, I "saw" a scene from Heaven. There was my mother, walking with the Savior, beside the crystal sea. And she was talking to Him about me! I saw how well He listened, with great attentiveness. And I realized then that my mother was simply doing what she had always done, talking to Him about me, only now He was there beside her. She could see His face and hear His voice. And she could know immediately His answers to her requests.

That mental picture, that spiritual "revelation," has sustained me all the years since. I live without her presence now, but not without her prayers. There's no need to say:

Forget Me Not

Just holding close the Bible that
　　Once knew her tender touch,
And tracing there the verses which
　　To her had meant so much,
I feel again the comfort of
　　My mother's constant care,
And how her every thought of me
　　Was turned into a prayer.

She knew that life was bound to bring
　　Some sorrow and some rain . . .
But while she could she shielded me
　　From heartaches and from pain.
She sang the well-remembered hymns,

And read to me the Word . . .
Then lovingly she took my hand
　And led me to the Lord.
She placed my tiny hand in His
　And looked into His face . . .
"I'll tend this child of Yours, dear Lord,
　And watch her grow in grace!"
She labored in that work of love
　For fifty years, and more . . .
Until she left this earthly place
　For Heaven's golden shore!

So now she walks along beside
　The Man of Galilee,
And as they talk, she frequently
　Reminds the Lord of me!
She tells Him of my latest need,
　(As if He didn't know) . . .
And pleads with Him to help me through
　My weariness and woe.

A sweet compassion fills His face,
　As Mother takes my part . . .
Because He loved *His* mother so
　He listens with His heart.
He vows the burdens she's revealed
　Will not so heavy be . . .
And here below I feel them lift,
　For they belonged to me.

And so when paths I take are right
   Or plans are richly blessed,
I know He's given honor to
   My mother's quiet request.
Altho' she lives in other worlds
   It's clear that still she cares . . .
I live without her presence now,
   But not without her prayers!

Echoes

I can hear the harmony
Even now . . .
The old treadmill sewing machine
Humming along as she sang
To herself . . .
"Jesus is near
To comfort and cheer
Just when I need Him
Most . . ."
And as a child
I would wonder if He
Was standing right beside her.

Now I know . . .
For I, too, have found Him there,
His hand on my shoulder,
And so will
My own daughter,
　And her daughter,
　　And her daughter . . .

Faith of our
Mothers . . .
Living still!

Wayward Child

A poignant page from our national history will always be the one written during the hostage crisis in Iran during 1978 and 1979. After 444 days the American men and women for whom the world had been so concerned were freed. As we watched their happy homecoming, their buoyant, boisterous welcome, the nation was collectively humming a little tune: "Tie a yellow ribbon 'round the old oak tree!" The inspiration for that song, sung by the musical star Tony Orlando, was supposedly a story published in *The New York Post* in 1971, in an article written by the award-winning columnist Pete Hamill. And perhaps that *is* the story that the songwriter of the '70s saw!

But long before Pete Hamill was a columnist, and long before Tony Orlando was singing songs, my mother was telling a version of that story to me, as an illustration of the love and forgiveness of God.

Mother's story came from the days of the Great Depression, a time with which my parents were well acquainted, for they were seminary students during those days of destitution for the entire nation.

In November of 1930 the bare, bleak lands of West Texas had never looked so desolate, as a single train, made up of a few creaky cars, whistle-stopped its way across the range. Inside the passenger car there were only two people, an elderly minister near the back, and a young man near the front. The young man wore clothing that was clean, but frayed and worn, like the worried look on his face. Finally, the old minister moved forward to sit beside him.

"Son," he said, "I'm a preacher of the Word, and I've learned, in my life, how to listen. Would you like to tell me why you are so worried?"

Tears began to roll down the rough young cheeks as the boy began to talk. "I left home, oh, it seems like a lifetime ago that I left home. And I left behind me all I'd been taught . . . the Good Book, the preachin', the prayin'. I tried to live without it. I thought I could. But I got into trouble . . . terrible, terrible trouble . . . and finally found myself in jail. It broke my mother's heart, Reverend, just broke her heart with me in jail. She cried and cried. I know she did because when her letters came, the words would be all smeared with tears. I could see the sadness was weighing her down. I thought it best if she just forgot me and my trouble. So I sent the last letters back, unopened, like I didn't want them.

"But, oh, Reverend, I've changed my mind. I'm free now, and I want more than anything I can think of to go home. But maybe *she* doesn't want *me* now. Maybe she can't forgive me. After what I've done, I'd understand if she didn't want to see me, didn't want me to stay around, you know?

"So I wrote her a letter last week, and I told her I was gettin' out. This train passes by our old home place . . . the farm, the house, the barn . . . and out back behind the barn there's this old oak tree where I used to climb up high and wave to the engineers as the trains went by. Well, Reverend, I told my ma, I'll be on the 6:30 train next Sunday evening, passing by our place. And if maybe you could let me come home, if maybe you could forgive me, then tie a white handkerchief on one of the branches of that old oak tree behind the barn. If it's there, I'll get off at the station and come on home. But if it's not, I'll just keep on riding into the night! That's what I told her, Reverend. That's what I told my ma. It's not far now. Just around that next hill up there, and we should be able to see it!"

The old preacher sat, praying silently, as the young man strained forward to see through the gathering dusk. And then they both gasped out loud!

The train rounded the hill, and there was the little farm, the house, the pasture, the barn. But it was the old oak tree that lighted up the landscape . . . for from every branch, from top to bottom, there hung not a handkerchief, but a *bedsheet*, waving in the breeze, bringing a wayward boy home!

As my mother would tell me this story, always with a tear or two, she would say, "So you see, this is like God's love, and His forgiveness toward us!" And as a child, in my mind's eye, I could see God's bedsheets waving from the branches of a tree beside the River Jordan . . . welcoming me home!

It is a "welcome scene" of which I would not have been aware, except for the bedtime storyteller, called Mother!

Surprise!

I remember vividly
That day in third grade
When I realized (with a start)
That I was not the
Prettiest, smartest,
Cutest little girl
In class.

MERCY!
Mother was wrong!

Mother's Husband

I was always "Daddy's girl." I must have looked a lot like him, because people I didn't even know connected us when they saw me. He loved music, and I did, too. He loved mischief, and I did, too. He loved people, and I did, too.

We were a family of readers. Most Saturdays we took a picnic lunch and folding wooden rockers out to the lake, where we read books together. I took my turn at reading a chapter even when I was still in grade school. I was nine years old when we read *Gone with the Wind*. Back then I was a skinny kid, with a long face and long brown hair that was straight as a board (when the style was curly). I knew I'd never be as pretty as Scarlett, but Daddy said I had more sense!

Well, soon I grew up some more, and was reasonably pretty . . . and thank goodness I still have more sense than Scarlett!

When I fell in love, Daddy was there for me as usual. He borrowed money to give me the wedding I wanted, and a year later drove through hail and high water, literally through a storm, to see my firstborn. What a lovely, laughing, kind man he was.

That's another thing Mother did for me . . . she chose Daddy. And their romance lasted a lifetime!

This is their . . .

Love Story

They always felt it was meant to be,
   The way they happened to meet . . .
And when they found they had fallen in love
   They had the whole world at their feet!
He sang and danced to the music he made
   And vowed they would never part . . .
She laughed, delighted, and called her love
   "The boy with a song in his heart"!
The candles burned in the little church
   When they became man and wife . . .
The flames reflected the look of love
   For now they were linked for life!
The children came, and the circle grew,
   When they bowed their heads to say grace . . .
And home was a harbor away from the storm
   As they anchored their lives in that place.
They had their share of trouble and trial,
   But gratefully counted the years . . .
Tho' sometimes the way seemed long and hard,
   There was always more laughter than tears.
She hardly noticed when time had turned,
   That his eyes were a little dim . . .

It mattered not that she used a cane
As long as she walked with him!

But then one day at twilight time,
   When the shadows were growing deep . . .
He said good-night in his loving way,
   And slipped away in his sleep.
The music stopped in her world that day,
Oh, how much she missed the song . . .
The days were silent without his voice,
   And the nights were all so long.
As she slept the sound of angel's wings
   Seemed soft, and hauntingly near,
For scenes of Heaven had filled her dreams . . .
   It was home to someone so dear!

But she prayed for strength to go on with life,
   To bear the being alone . . .
And bravely she walked with a smile on her lips
   Til at last the Lord said, "Come home!"
The years fell away as she stood to go . . .
   So young she felt, and so free!
She heard then the *music* she missed so much,
   The same joyful melody!
Like a girl she ran to the Golden Gates,
   To love that would never depart . . .
For waiting there, with his arms open wide,
Was the boy with a song in his heart!

A Red Rose

It was Mother's Day,
And as we left the little church
There were two baskets by the door . . .
One of red roses, one of white,
A gift for each worshiper . . .
A red rose for those
Whose mothers were living,
And white for those
Whose mothers were not.

I stood beside the white roses,
For my mother had been
In heaven for many years . . .
But suddenly I reached
Into the other basket
And took a red rose!

She is more real to me
Now than ever, I thought . . .
Each time I give my love,
Guide my children,
Guard my values,

Instinctively touch
My husband's heart . . .
I remember Mother!
She taught me,
Led me,
Shaped my life
So lovingly!
Her memory lives . . .

And my rose is red!

JOY DAVIS is a popular public speaker, filling more than 100 engagements each year. She often dramatizes the plots of great books for women's clubs, book clubs, women's forums, and brings inspirational messages to Christian women's retreats. She has received numerous awards, including the George Washington Honor Medal from the Freedom Foundation in Valley Forge. Joy has been listed in *Personalities of the South* and in *Who's Who of American Women*.

Joy has written eight books, including two children's books, and five collections of poetry. Her poetry has been endorsed by America's favorite commentator, Paul Harvey, who has read from her collections several times on his national broadcasts. Further endorsements have come from several best-selling Christian authors and speakers, including Florence Littauer, Luci Swindol, Barbara Johnson, and Ruth Graham.

Joy is married to Jewell A. Davis, a retired aeronautical engineer. They live in Dallas, Texas.